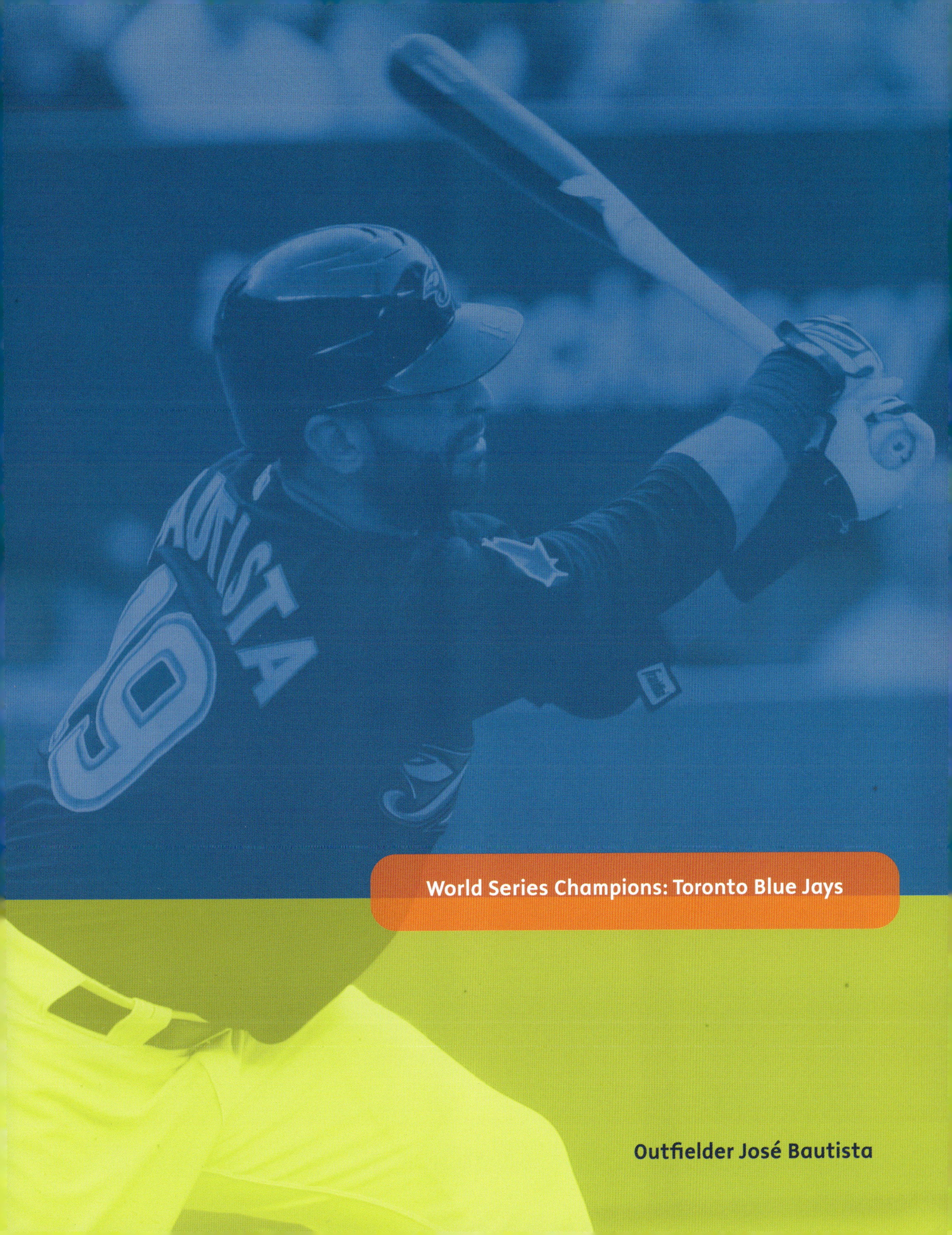

World Series Champions: Toronto Blue Jays

Outfielder José Bautista

Pitcher Alek Manoah

WORLD SERIES CHAMPIONS

TORONTO BLUE JAYS

MICHAEL E. GOODMAN

CREATIVE SPORTS

CREATIVE EDUCATION / CREATIVE PAPERBACKS

Published by Creative Education and Creative Paperbacks
P.O. Box 227, Mankato, Minnesota 56002
Creative Education and Creative Paperbacks are imprints of The Creative Company
www.thecreativecompany.us

Art Direction by Tom Morgan
Book production by Ciara Beitlich
Edited by Joe Tischler

Photographs by Alamy (Zuma Press, Inc.), AP Images (Julian Avram/Icon Sportswire, Julio Cortez), Corbis (Rich Pilling), Getty (Bettmann, Mark Blinch, Lisa Blumenfeld, Stephen Dunn, Focus on Sport, Getty Images Sport, Craig Melvin/Stringer, Rich Pilling, Rick Stewart/Stringer), Shutterstock (Lucky-photographer)

Library of Congress Cataloging-in-Publication Data
Names: Goodman, Michael E., author.
Title: Toronto Blue Jays / Michael E. Goodman.
Description: Mankato, MN : Creative Education and Creative Paperbacks, [2024] | Series: Creative sports. World Series champions | Includes index. | Audience: Ages 7-10 | Audience: Grades 2-3 | Summary: "Elementary-level text and engaging sports photos highlight the Toronto Blue Jays' MLB World Series wins, plus sensational players associated with the professional baseball team such as Vladimir Guerrero, Jr."--Provided by publisher.
Identifiers: LCCN 2023011822 (print) | LCCN 2023011823 (ebook) | ISBN 9781640268364 (library binding) | ISBN 9781682773864 (paperback) | ISBN 9781640269897 (pdf)
Subjects: LCSH: Toronto Blue Jays (Baseball team)--History--Juvenile literature. | World Series (Baseball)--History--Juvenile literature.
Classification: LCC GV875.T67 G67 2024 (print) | LCC GV875.T67 (ebook) | DDC 796.357/6409713541--dc23/eng/20220314
LC record available at https://lccn.loc.gov/2023011822
LC ebook record available at https://lccn.loc.gov/2023011823

Printed in China

1993 World Series Champions

Pitcher Ricky Romero

CONTENTS

Home of the Blue Jays

Toronto is the largest city in Canada. It is located near Lake Ontario. Nearby is a **stadium** called Rogers Centre. The Blue Jays baseball team plays there. They are the only Major League Baseball (MLB) team to play its home games outside the United States.

The Toronto Blue Jays compete in the American League (AL) East Division. Their biggest **rivals** are the Tampa Bay Rays. All MLB teams want to win the World Series and become champions.

Pitcher Juan Guzmán

Naming the Blue Jays

Team owners asked fans to suggest a name for the new club. "Blue Jays" got a lot of votes. One fan wrote, "I hope players hit the ball as fast as a jay can fly." The team is often called "Jays," for short.

Pitcher Dave Stieb

Blue Jays History

The Blue Jays were added to the AL in 1977. They lost a lot of games at first. The team got better after second baseman Dámaso García and pitcher Dave Stieb arrived. In 1983, they led the Jays to their first winning season. Two years later, the team made the **playoffs** for the first time.

In 1989, Cito Gaston was named team manager. He quickly led the Jays to the top of the AL East. In 1992, they rose even higher. They defeated the Atlanta Braves to win their first World Series crown. Starting pitcher Jimmy Key had two wins in the series. Toronto fans got another thrill in 1993. A **walk-off home run** by outfielder Joe Carter made the Jays champs again!

Outfielder Joe Carter

Pitcher Roy Halladay

The Jays have not won any more **titles**. But they have continued to have strong pitching and power hitting. Righties Pat Hentgen, Roger Clemens, and Roy Halladay each won a Cy Young Award. The best pitchers win them. Sluggers Carlos Delgado and José Bautista hit a lot of home runs.

In 2015, third baseman Josh Donaldson powered the Jays to the playoffs again. Donaldson was voted AL Most Valuable Player (MVP).

Other Blue Jays Stars

Second baseman Roberto Alomar was a great fielder and hitter for the Jays. He was elected to the Baseball **Hall of Fame**. He wore his Blue Jays hat when he got his award. He wanted to show how proud he was to be part of the team.

In the 1980s, Jays outfielder George Bell was an AL All-Star. So were Lloyd Moseby and Jesse Barfield.

Second baseman Roberto Alomar

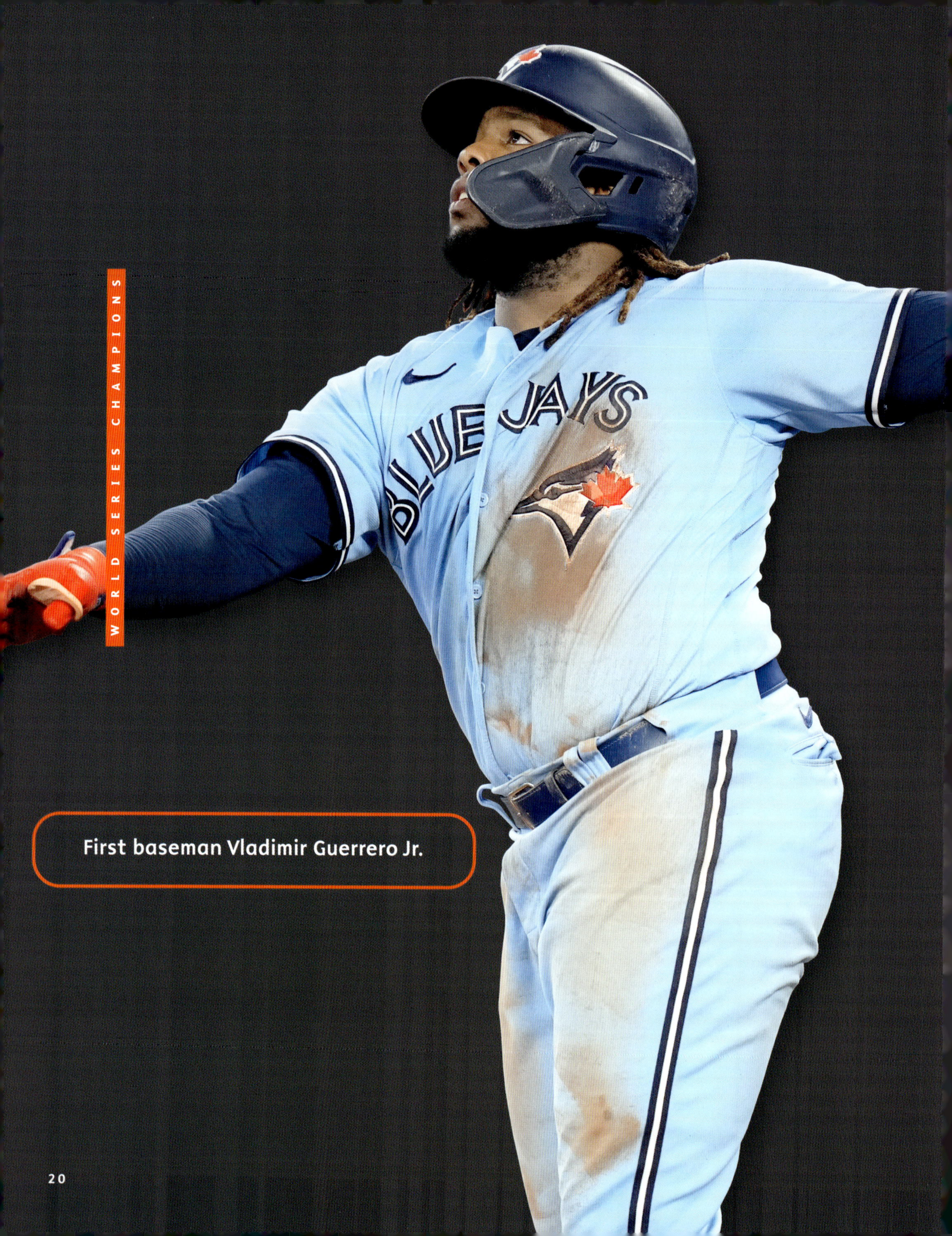

First baseman Vladimir Guerrero Jr.

The Blue Jays have made the playoffs four times since 2015. Toronto fans are counting on new stars Vladimir Guerrero Jr. and Alek Manoah. Fans hope they will bring home another championship soon!

About the Blue Jays

Started playing: 1977

League/division: American League, East Division

Team colors: royal blue, navy blue, and red

Home stadium: Rogers Centre

WORLD SERIES CHAMPIONSHIPS:

1992, 4 games to 2 over Atlanta Braves

1993, 4 games to 2 over Philadelphia Phillies

Toronto Blue Jays website: www.mlb.com/bluejays

Glossary

Hall of Fame—a museum in which the best players of all time are honored

playoffs—games that the best teams play after a regular season to see who the champion will be

rival—a team that plays extra hard against another team

stadium—a building with tiers of seats for spectators

title—another word for championship

walk-off home run—a home run hit in the bottom of the ninth or in extra innings that gives the home team the win, ending the game

Outfielder Lloyd Moseby

Index